Heian Honto

Decoding the self-defence syllabus contained in the Heian kata series

Copyright © 2022-2023 Pete Cordell
All rights reserved.
This book or any portion thereof may not be reproduced or used in any manner whatsoever without the express written permission of the author except for the use of brief quotations with accompanying references.
Revision 9.

Contents

Introduction 3

Background, Principles and Concepts 5

Heian Shodan 23

Heian Nidan 37

Heian Sandan 47

Heian Yondan 61

Heian Godan 75

Conclusion 89

References 93

Introduction

I gained my 1st Dan in Korean karate in 2016. Like many new Black Belts, I then asked myself the question, "what next?"

Gaining your Black Belt offers you the opportunity to look beyond the syllabus and explore where you'd like to direct your martial arts energies next. As an aging karateka I was not going to have a future in competition. I'm still not particularly good at sparring. So I decided to explore kata. Particularly the Japanese katas that I hadn't covered in my Korean style.

The Internet, and YouTube in particular, is a great tool for this type of self-study. As I explored kata videos I came across many that included in the title the words "... with bunkai" [Bunkai] (Note: All references are listed at the back of the book). If you've picked up this book, you will likely know that "bunkai" roughly means "application". In essence, "what do the moves in the kata represent".

Exploring the YouTube comments (not usually a worthwhile exercise!), I came across references to the work of Iain Abernethy [Jutsu], and from there into the history of karate and what some call "Applied Karate" or "Practical Karate". This led me to reflect on the Korean katas that I had already learnt.

In the process of decoding the Korean Palgue katas from an "Applied Karate" perspective I was blown away by how well the katas were constructed and the clever syllabus they represented. I felt compelled to write down what I had deduced so that future generations of karateka could have the opportunity to marvel at the genius of these katas' authors as I have done [Palgue].

Having explored the Korean Palgue katas I started looking at the Japanese Heian katas. The Korean karatekas who developed the Palgue kata series studied under Funakoshi who was responsible for much of the specifics of how the Heian kata are performed today. I was interested to find out if the Palgue katas were an evolution of the Heian katas and whether the Heian katas could be decomposed into a similar syllabus. This book is the result of that analysis.

Background, Principles and Concepts

But first, let's take a step back. Why is kata a thing and why do we do it? Let's have a look at a simplified history of karate and kata.

The fighting techniques that evolved into karate emerged in China and crossed into the Japanese island of Okinawa as a result of trade via shipping. Many styles developed, with more or less cross-fertilisation on an ad-hoc basis.

Before YouTube and widespread literacy, the method adopted for recording fighting techniques was kata. For this reason, kata is often called the textbook of karate. A key task of an instructor is to mould their students into a new copy of the style's textbook, and part of the black belt grading is to ensure that the students are a sufficiently good copy of the textbook. This is one of the reasons why kata plays such a big part in karate.

Early styles often focussed around a single kata. It was very rare for someone to know more than two or three. Funakoshi, the founder of the Shotokan style of karate, is said to have spent three years learning the kata Kiba Dachi Shodan (also known as Teki Shodan and similar to Naihanchi) before he was allowed to attempt the next kata in the series.

One of Funakoshi's teachers was Itosu. At the beginning of the 1900s, Itosu convinced the authorities to introduce karate into schools as a form of physical education. The focus was put more on physical conditioning, self-control and discipline rather than pure combat effectiveness. As part of this, he felt that the traditional katas were too complicated for children to learn. Legend has it that he therefore broke the longer, and more difficult, Kusanku (also known as Kanku Dai) into 5 parts to form the Pinan series of katas. Others theorise that the Pinan series is based on multiple katas and may even have multiple authors. Either way, the key innovation is having multiple related katas instead of one long kata.

However Itosu developed the Pinan katas, it is clear that he essentially started with a clean sheet of paper. He could pull in parts of other katas that represented the techniques that he wanted to convey and also modify or completely invent moves as he saw necessary. Importantly, developing five katas instead of one offered the opportunity for a great deal of material and, as I hope to show in the book, offered the opportunity to partition the material into sections that covered different aspects of self-defence.

Pinan is a Chinese word and Funakoshi changed the name to Heian to make it more Japanese friendly. He also modified the Pinan katas in small ways, including swapping the order of the first two katas around as he thought that made for an easier progression from easy to difficult.

Itosu (and Funakoshi) promoted teaching karate as part of the school curriculum. To make the kata acceptable to the authorities in that environment (and presumably parents!) Itosu toned down the explanations of the kata moves. The bunkai was mainly described as a series of blocks and counter punches. It is for this reason that many karateka consider the Heian series as merely a form of kids' aerobics and not worth teaching to adults. However, Itosu also taught the kata to adults to whom it is known he taught a more practical bunkai [NotKids]. Alas, it is the bunkai taught to kids that we are most familiar with these days and karateka have been attempting to divine the adult bunkai ever since! I hope to show in this book that the Heian series is worthy of study by adults.

The first thing that becomes apparent when we start trying to understand kata rather than merely reproduce them, is that they are like onions: They have layers.

As described by Iain Abernethy [Abernethy], there is the analysing part (Bunkai/Bunseki) of kata and then there is the practical part (Oyo). There is also Omote and Ura. Omote and Ura are two sides to the same medal in the Japanese culture. Omote is the obvious and Ura is the hidden introverted side.

YouTuber Jesse Enkamp, AKA The Karate Nerd, divides kata interpretations into Omote, Ura and Honto [Enkamp]. Omote is the surface interpretation. If a downward block is performed, then a downward block is the interpretation. Ura means backside, back or reverse. We see it in the kick name "Ura Mawashi Geri" (Reverse Roundhouse Kick). Here a downward block can become a strike to the groin. Honto means truth. In this interpretation, rather than being a block or a strike, a downward block can be interpreted as something quite different, such as an armlock.

In this book we will be doing Bunkai (analysing) of the Ura and Honto aspects of the katas' Oyo (application).

Thus we finally come to the topic of this book: A honto interpretation of the Heian kata series - Heian Honto.

Rules

If kata is the textbook of karate then the moves within them are the words. In the same way that sheet music is a notation for music, the moves within kata are a notation for fighting moves. The difference between sheet music and real music is large. The difference between kata moves and real fighting moves is much smaller. But there is still often a difference between the notation and what they represent, and this must be remembered when interpreting the kata.

To help with decoding the notation the Gōjū-ryū style of karate has a set of rules for interpreting kata [Rules]:

Three basic rules - *Shuyo san gensoko*

1. Don't be deceived by the shape (embusen) of the kata.

    The kata embusen is designed to allow the kata to be performed within a small space. The shape of the embusen has no bearing on the meaning of the techniques in the kata.

2. Techniques executed while advancing are offensive. Those executed while retreating are defensive.

3. There is only one opponent and he is in front of you.

    Turning to face a new direction while performing the kata *does not* mean you are turning to face a new opponent.

Advanced rules - *Hosoku joko*

1. Every movement in kata is significant and is to be used in application.

   There are no "salutation", religious or empty movements in kata. *All* movements in the kata have meaning.

2. A closed pulling hand returning to chamber usually has some part of the opponent in it.

   When pulling a hand to the chamber position (such as on the hip), particularly if it is closed, it should be considered to have some part of the opponent in its grip. e.g. an arm, wrist or even head.

3. Utilize the shortest distance to your opponent.

   The kata will typically attack the opponent with the closest part of your body.

4. If you control an opponent's head you control the opponent.

   Kata techniques often target vital or weak points of the body (Kyusho), many of the most important of these are in the head. e.g. eyes or throat.

5. There are no blocks.

   Uke are not blocks, they are "defences", however in kata they may not even represent defences, but simply be the movements of the limbs required to execute a more complex technique like a throw.

6. Angles in kata are very important.

    The angle to which you turn represents the angle which you must take relative to the opponent for the technique to work. It *does not* represent turning to face a new opponent.

7. Touching your own body in kata indicates that you are touching part of your opponent.

    In the absence of a partner to practice with, where the kata touches your own body, you would be touching or holding part of the opponent's body.

8. Don't attack hard parts of your opponent with hard parts of your body.

    The kata typically strikes hard parts of the opponent with soft parts of your body and soft parts with hard parts of your body.

9. There are no pauses in the application.

    The rhythm of the performance of kata has no bearing on the performance of the techniques extracted from it.

Note that Advanced Rule 6, "Angles in kata are very important", appears to contradict Simple Rule 1, "Don't be deceived by the shape (embusen) of the kata". Clearly some changes of direction are more important than others. In the Heian series, the majority of changes of direction are simply to fit the kata within a reasonable floor area. What is significant is each kata contains a number of combinations. Changes of direction often mark the beginning and end of combinations. Thus a change of direction at the start of a combination doesn't immediately suggest taking on an angle relative to an opponent. The new combination represents dealing with an opponent under different circumstances, not moving on to attacking a new opponent having completed dealing with the first. Conversely, a change of direction within a combination typically represents changing position relative to a single opponent, not moving on to another opponent.

Advanced Rule 5 says "There are no blocks". This doesn't mean you shouldn't do blocks. Blocks in an application are done on an as-needed basis. A kata may restrict the options that an opponent has to counter but it can't anticipate all actions of an opponent. Hence, in an application you may have to block mid-way through a combination, or even abandon a combination entirely and start a new one, due to the actions of the opponent. The exception I make to this is a block at the start of a combination that directly leads on to a technique that either strikes or controls the opponent. For example, a block may lead to a wrist grab which is then pulled back to the hip to restrict the movement of the opponent. In that way, a kata can tell you that if you find yourself doing a particular block, what techniques follow on fluidly from there.

Another important consideration is, as mentioned earlier, kata is the textbook of karate. Each person that learns the katas is a new copy of the textbook. They will hopefully go on to teach others to be copies of the textbook. This means that the katas have to be designed in such a way that they can be copied time and time again without any loss of fidelity. Those of a certain age will be familiar with the issue of loss of fidelity caused by copying from using cassette tapes and photocopying. For example, having a move that is best performed at an angle of 78.3° to the attacker can't be represented in the kata so specifically because people are not very good a measuring such angles with sufficient precision. As more copies of the kata are made, the represented angle would drift. And you have to remember that the optimum angle of a technique may depend on the person performing the technique, the person that the technique is being performed on and even the terrain the technique is performed on. To address this, the katas round the various angles to ones that can be more easily represented, such as 90° and 45°.

Funakoshi wrote in [MyWay]:

> "The Japanese language is not an easy one to master, nor is it always quite so explicit as it might be: different characters may have exactly the same pronunciation, and a single character may have different pronunciation, depending upon the use."

The same can be said about the language of kata. A move in one place in a kata may have a different meaning to the same move elsewhere in the kata or in a different kata. English also has this property. Take the word "light". It has a number of meanings. It can mean not heavy, light as in light from the Sun, a light as in a light bulb, and you can light a fire. We can work out which meaning is intended from the context. It's for this reason I prefer a kata to have a theme that binds all the bunkai together – so all the moves have the same or similar context. I consider a bunkai to be better if adjacent combinations have similar interpretations. Often this means a subsequent combination will describe a situation where an earlier combination was not appropriate or wasn't possible to fully complete for some reason. A "better bunkai" will be one where subsequent combinations are "Plan B"s to earlier "Plan A"s. I believe the Heian series demonstrates this very well.

Another observation in this vein is that small variations to the spelling of the word "light" yield significantly different meanings. For example, "flight", "plight", "delight", "might" and "sight" are all similar to "light" in spelling but have very different meanings. Thus we do need to be aware of small movements that may invalidate our bunkai. Against that, we know, as with regular languages, kata moves have changed over time, sometimes to more closely represent someone's favourite bunkai which may actually differ from the originally intended bunkai. Additionally, it's worth noting that many languages have regional dialects meaning that the same concept can be expressed in different ways. (For example, "lite" in place of "light".) Kata is likely to be similar, meaning that moves from kata from different regions can't necessarily be interpreted the same way.

Egyptian hieroglyphs can also teach us something about interpreting kata. On first looking at Egyptian hieroglyphs you might assume it only captures information about animals and agriculture, whereas it is actually a full and complete language that uses depictions of animals and agriculture to represent higher level concepts. Kata is essentially a language of blocks, punches and kicks. This is good because most of what it has to convey is about blocks, punches and kicks. But sometimes it needs to convey other information, but it is still restricted to the medium of blocks, punches and kicks, and we need to bear this in mind when analysing kata. So, for example, we might initially assume a punch represents a punch, but if the punch doesn't fit well within the interpretation we must be prepared to consider that the punch represents something else, such as a grab.

In all of this, it is important to be careful to avoid treating particular bunkai as either right or wrong. Similarly it is important to avoid talking about "the" bunkai as if it is the only valid bunkai. I do consider certain bunkai to be better than others because I believe it is closer to what the kata creator(s) intended for those particular moves (which is deduced by the surmised common context). But that doesn't mean that bunkai that the kata creator didn't intend is without value. If some kata moves remind you of certain techniques, that you can then practice or teach, then the bunkai is useful and therefore valuable.

For this reason I like to divide bunkai into primary bunkai and secondary bunkai. The primary bunkai is my best guess at what the kata creator originally intended. As stated above, this depends on how well it fits in with the rest of the kata theme, and there is usually only one primary bunkai for a set of moves. My primary bunkai may actually change over time as I further analyse a kata. The secondary bunkai is all the other techniques that those moves remind me of. Referring back to above, they correspond not only to the different definitions of "light" but also to the different spelling variations such as "flight" and "plight". Hence when talking about bunkai it's appropriate to say, "This is my primary bunkai, but there are also these cool secondary bunkais to look at." (Note, not "...the primary bunkai..." as we will likely never truly know "the" primary bunkai). It's also appropriate to say, "I don't have a primary bunkai for that, but here are some secondary bunkai."

In this book I describe my primary bunkai for the Heian kata series. I hope I can convince you to adopt it as your primary bunkai.

Shorthand

One thing I have found when reading books on kata is that it is very hard to follow a kata simply from written words. This book does not seek to teach the katas, but it is important to be able to know which part of a kata is being discussed.

The hardest part in my experience is working out which part of the kata is being discussed. To help with this I have devised a simple, concise notation for various moves in kata. This is as follows:

=	Ready stance - Yoi
< or > followed by a number	Turn to the left ("<") or right (">") by the indicated number of degrees. For example, "<90" means turns left 90 degrees. Bear in mind that most turns start with the front leg except the 270° turns which start with the back leg.
^	Indicates a move forward.
v	Move backwards.
N, S, E, W	The direction you are facing relative to compass coordinates. You always start facing North, represented by "N". If you left 90° you will be facing West, represented by "W".
\ or /	Indicates a forward stance (zenkutsu-dachi), either left foot forwards ("\") or right foot forwards ("/"). To understand this notation, imagine you are standing on the page, looking to the top

	of the page. Your front foot is positioned on the top of the symbol and your back foot on the bottom.
] or [	Indicates a back stance (kokutsu-dachi), with back foot pointing left ("]") or back foot facing right ("["). To understand this notation, imagine you are standing on the page, looking to the top of the page. The bottom of the symbol indicates the direction your back foot is pointing. Ignore the mark at the top of the symbol!
_	(Underscore) Horse stance (kiba-dachi)
{}	I put the move description in curly braces to separate them from the rest of the description. E.g. {downward block}
...	A pause or space between moves.
*	Kiai (Shout)

For example, the first few moves of Heian Shodan are represented by:

= N ...
<90 W \ {downward block} ...
^ / {punch body} ...
>180 E / {downward block} ...

That all means, start in Yoi (Ready stance) facing North. Turn left 90° to face West into a forward stance with downward block. Move forwards in forward stance with punch body. Turn right 180° to face East into forward stance with downward block and so on.

When explaining the bunkai I sometimes include the relevant kata moves in curly braces, (e.g. {downward block}), to help tie the bunkai to the kata.

I have chosen to use the English names for the techniques. I have done this to make the text more accessible to beginners and also for karateka that practice non-Japanese styles of karate. For practitioners of Japanese styles who are not familiar with English terminology, here is a list of the terms I use:

Downward block	gedan-barai
Side block	Either uchi-uke or soto-uke depending on style. For this book side block starts inside and moves to the outside. For example, the left fist goes first to the right hip and then blocks to the left.
Reinforced side block	morote-uke
Upper block	age-uke
Middle area block	Either soto-uke or uchi-uke depending on style. For this book middle area block starts outside and then moves to the centreline of the body. For example, the left fist starts to the left of the body and then blocks to the centreline of the body.

Knife hand block	shuto-uke
Hammer fist	tetsui-uchi
Vertical hammer fist	The fist moves vertically downwards usually from about nose height to chest height
Horizontal hammer fist	The fist is swung in the horizontal plane
Spear hand	nukite
Back fist	uraken. In the case of these katas the back fist is in the vertical plane, striking downwards
Elbow strike	empi-uchi
Punch body	oi-zuki
Punch head	
Reverse punch	gyaku-zuki
Front kick	mae-geri
Side kick	yoko-geri

Naturally when breaking down a kata I speak about combinations. Often a combination is performed first in one direction and then the mirror image is performed in the opposite direction. For the sake of brevity, rather than saying things like "skipping the mirror combination and moving onto the combination after that" I simply use the term "next different combination" or just "next combination". Hence, in Heian Nidan, having performed the initial combination to the west, I use "next combination" to mean moving onto the combination with the kick to the rear (south) rather than the mirrored combination to the east.

At the start of the discussion of each combination a small icon is shown. The icon shows the kata embusen with an arrowhead showing the position of the combination. In addition to showing where in the kata the combination appears, they also serve as a way of separating one combination's description from another. At Ready stance (Yoi) you start at the bottom of the icon, facing up the page. The icon for the first combination of Heian Shodan is:

Photos

The combination of being in a Coronavirus world and these katas not being those of my style has meant there are a lack of talented, good-looking victims that I can pick on to be in the photos. I have therefore stepped up to the plate and featured in them myself. As you can see, I am no Bruce Lee or Kanazawa, and it will be clear that this is not my style (which is way, following the lead of The Karate Nerd, I have chosen to wear a white belt in the kata photos). (Similarly it follows that if your instructor tells you to do the moves differently, do what they say rather than following the pictures in this book as they will be correct for your particular style. And if nothing else, they will be the ones grading you!)

Each photo is posed and taken with a still camera. I feel this has lost some fluidity in the bunkai photos. The kicks in the kata photos were a particular challenge for this old man, requiring a leg to be held in the air while the camera decided whether it could be bothered to take a photo or not.

We've attempted to photograph each combination from the side that shows most detail. Hence the effective viewpoint changes from combination to combination. This may mean you need to re-align your bearings when looking at each new combination.

I hope these physical and technical deficiencies do not detract from your enjoyment of this book.

Acknowledgements

I'd like to thank Iain Abernethy. Not only did his work start me on this path, he was very supportive of my Palgue kata series book [Palgue] (including offering very speedy feedback), which led to writing this book. It's important to make clear that I think what I present in this book may be deemed by many as "controversial" (which is part of the reason for writing it!) and I believe Iain has different interpretations to what I present here. So, if you don't like what I present here that is no reflection on Iain.

Another big thank you goes to Sensei Patrick McCarthy for giving his blessing to using the images from his [Bubishi] book used in the Heian Sandan chapter. I find it really satisfying to be able to use these images to show a connection between the ancient karate of the Bubishi and the modern karate we practice today.

Finally, I'd like to thank my sons Theo (attacker) and Joseph (photographer) for tolerating their father's obsession and helping me take the photos.

Heian Shodan
Striking Out

Let's jump straight in and look at the first combination of Heian Shodan:

= N ... <90 W \ {downward block} ... ^ / {punch body}

(From ready stance – yoi, turn left 90° to face west into forward stance with downward block, followed by step forward with punch body.)

This is usually presented as a block against an attacker's strike followed by a punch to the body. But is a downward block the most sensible suggestion for a block against an attacker's punch? A full kihon style downward block would cover most of the area that needed to be protected, but the fold required would take too long for it to be effective against a punch to the body and wouldn't protect against a punch to the head. As a first "go-to" block, something like a side block or upper block, would be a better recommendation for this first kata to make if this were the intended scenario. We need to consider alternatives.

So let's imagine the scene… you are in the streets and confronted, face-to-face by an attacker. If running away is still an option, it is the smart and courageous thing to do. You do this by turning to the right and legging it. If this is successful there are no further techniques required.

But what happens if the attempt to run away is not successful? We need to consider how the attacker stops you. Likely as you turn to the right the attacker will grab your left arm or shoulder using their right hand. If you're lucky, the attacker will step forward with their right foot.

This nicely opens the attacker up for you to turn to your left and do a downward block – to the attacker's groin (<90 W \ {downward block}).

Executed well, the attacker's response to this is reasonably predictable. Unless he has balls of steel, his reflex will be to clench tightly with his right hand, firmly holding on to the your arm, bend over slightly and twist away from you.

This opens the way for your next move – ^ / Pb. You step forward and punch. The punch in the kata is to body height, but because the attacker has bent over the target is now a knockout blow to the chin.

The pictures might appear to show striking the attacker in the groin and punching them in the head simply because they have grabbed your shoulder. You might think this is an excessive response, especially if you are familiar with "Karate ni sente nashi" or "There is no first strike in karate" [Twenty]. However, prior to this, words have been exchanged and you have attempted to escape. During your escape the attacker aggressively grabbed you and you can reasonably expect that their next move will be to strike you. Under this situation, when you have done all you can to avoid a fight, you can pre-emptively strike without waiting for the attacker to strike first. Iain Abernethy has written further on this at [Strike]. Whether it is intentional or coincidence, I like that the kata starts with this turn to the left because it gives the opportunity to bring up the subject of avoiding a fight if possible and when it is appropriate to pre-emptively strike.

If this combination is successful, this completes the instructions of the kata. There is no requirement for there to be another opponent behind you on whom you can perform a similar procedure. The rest of the kata describes situations when this move doesn't go to plan or it's not a suitable technique to use.

Let's look at them.

⊺→

>180 E / {downward block} ...
{right leg pulls back, right fist circles clockwise to vertical hammer fist} ...
^ / {punch body}

This combination is similar to the first but has the additional circular arm movement. The rationale often presented for this circular arm movement is that it is an escape from a grabbed wrist. To me, the idea that your arm is likely to get caught in a groin strike is unnecessarily pessimistic. And even if your hand does get grabbed, if your next move is a strike to the chin the fact that your non-punching arm has been grabbed is of no consequence. It is better to complete your strike before the attacker can counter-strike rather than spend time freeing your arm.

Instead, the circular arm movement is moving your arm around the attacker's bent body and grabbing their head, for example by the hair. This gives you control of their head, preventing them rotating their head too far away from you, and also gives you tactile feedback on the position of the head which makes the follow-on strike more likely to succeed.

In more detail, the initial horizontal part of the circular motion is actually the quick retraction of the fist after the groin strike. It is done at speed to avoid the attacker grabbing it. This example shows that the pauses in a kata are not necessarily pauses in application. A kata is akin to a series of still images of fluid action.

So the movement isn't a release from a grab. But escaping grabs is important and as they are not discussed elsewhere in the kata series it might be appropriate for an instructor to discuss them at this stage as an aside. Including such asides when describing a kata application shows how kata can be used as a framework for remembering and presenting material beyond what is primarily expressed in the kata.

The next combination starts as follows:

    <90 N \ {downward block} ...
    {upper block, hand open} ...
    ^ / {upper block, hand closed}

(Turn left 90 degrees to downward block, raise blocking arm to upper block position with hand open, then step forward with upper block.)

This is actually more similar to the second combination with the circular arm movement than you might initially think!

The downward block is the same, with the same intent. But in this case the strike is less successful, and the attacker does not end up bent over. As a consequence you have to reach up higher to grab the attacker's hair. The follow-on strike is necessarily different also. Because the attacker is likely to end up more face-on giving a less ideal opportunity for a forward strike to the chin, the forearm is used to strike to the attacker's neck and under their chin.

The remaining upper blocks in this combination repeat this grab – strike sequence. (Although grab – strike, strike, strike is also viable or maybe even preferable. There's no point in releasing the grab if you don't have to!) Subsequent grabs may be grabbing the head as before or clearing out arms that are getting in the way of the strikes.

While the kata shows the strikes as upper blocks (perhaps not to alarm the kids' parents!), elbow strikes or any other such technique that does the job can be substituted. This is an example of a kata showing a principle where variations of the techniques shown are permissible in practice.

This application also shows one reason why the rising arm in a Japanese upper block goes outside of the returning arm. The returning arm in pulling the head forward and the rising arm is striking at the neck, which is further away.

Moving on...

There's repetition in the next downward block, punch sequences so I'll skip the:

    <270 E \ {downward block} ... ^ / {punch body} ...
    >180 W / {downward block} ... ^ \ {punch body}

And move on to the next combination...

<90 S \ {downward block} ... ^ / {punch body} ... ^ \ {punch} ... ^ / {punch}

At first glance this looks like a lot of punches. However, as you know, the timing of the punches isn't even. I learnt it as slow, quick, quick. In [Kyōhan], Funakoshi says:

> "When you repeat the same technique or movement three times, you must distinguish each one by doing it with varying degrees of power and strength. In other words, the first time, do the movement with power and strength. The second time you do it with less power and strength, and then the third time you once again do it with strength and power."

If all three punches were simply brute force strikes, why would you hold back on the second punch? The situation is that this leg is actually two combinations and I think it is best to think of the punches as powerful, quick, powerful.

The first combination is made up of the downward block and first punch. When you are near your attacker, you grab their right hand with your left hand and then punch to the solar plexus with your right hand.

The subsequent two punches are when you start further from your attacker. The quick punch is a reach with your left hand to your attacker's right hand. This is done with speed with no need for power. The following powerful punch is to the solar plexus as before.

This may seem an alien technique to modern karateka but below is a photo of Funakoshi instructing just such a technique.

↰

The final combination in the kata is:

<270 W [{knife hand} … >45] NW {knife hand}

This is a repetition of the grab and strike principle. You are again grabbing with your left hand, but this time you are grabbing the attacker's left hand and then pulling them across the front of your body. This makes it harder for the attacker to strike you with their free hand. You then strike over the attacker's left arm with your right arm to the attacker's neck.

A change of body angle is often interpreted in bunkai as taking up a new position relative to the attacker. Here the explanation is simpler. By moving the shoulders 45 degrees to the attacker, the target neck area is in the middle of the arc of the striking arm rather than at the end, making the strike easier and more effective.

To summarise, the topic of this kata is striking with limb (or head) control. I believe this is one of the defining features of karate. Boxing is purely punching, whereas the likes of aikido and jujitsu and primarily limb control. Employing striking with limb control separates karate from the other fighting arts.

A number of karateka criticise karate for placing the non-punching hand on the hip when we do basics (kihon) rather than keeping it up to our head as a guard. This kata clearly explains why we do that. It is to control our attacker and ideally move them into a position where they can't strike back.

This reminds me of the Western forces' tactics in the Iraq war. The goal of the first airstrikes was to take out Iraqi defences so that Iraqi forces could not counter strike. Only when the Western forces had removed the threat of counter strikes did they attack more significant targets. This demonstrates that this principle applies equally from individual fighting all the way up to large scale military campaigns. This is very satisfying as Japanese military authors such as Sun Tzu [ArtWar] and Musashi [5Rings] often present combat principles as universally applicable between the individual situation and large-scale military manoeuvres. "*This should be considered carefully.*"

It can be seen that this kata offers a very good lesson plan. Rather than just teaching the moves of the kata, the material could be taught and practiced over a number of lessons. For each combination, first demonstrate the moves from the kata and then do some partner exercises to experiment with the principles illustrated by the combination. This gives a deeper understanding of the kata and also helps with learning the moves.

This kata also demonstrates another benefit of bunkai. When I first leant Heian Shodan, all those repetitive downward block / punches made the kata mind numbingly boring, and it felt like an insult to my intelligence. My main thought when performing it was just to get it over with so I could move on to the next one. Once you have a bunkai for each move, the kata becomes more interesting. As you perform the kata you can imagine your opponent in front of you and focus on each application, allowing you to immerse yourself deeper in the kata and giving you a focus to improve your performance. Having an attacking bunkai rather than a defensive bunkai encourages you to put power into your execution, not only making the kata look better, but also maximising the physical benefit of performing the kata.

Heian Nidan
Second or First Kata?

⟻

{drop into back stance facing west,
    simultaneously do left side block with back of hand facing back and right upper block} ...
{simultaneously left arm pulls in, right arm drops down then upper cut} ...
{simultaneously left arm hammer fist to left, right fist to right hip}

There are many applications for this set of moves. When selecting an application in this context it is worth remembering that this is the first combination in Itosu's original Pinan series (Remember that Funakoshi swapped the order of the first two katas). Therefore, it seems unlikely that it will be one of the throws described in

[Kyōhan] which involve picking up your attacker, rotating them round and dropping them on their head.

Here you are being attacked from the side. Rather than pausing to turn and face your attacker before countering as they would expect, you catch them by surprise by shifting sideways, putting your left arm behind their back and grabbing their hair or something similar with your right hand. You pull their head and body down, release the right hand and bring it round to do an "upper cut" punch to the solar plexus. You then return your dazed attacker to a standing position and firmly hold them in place. If the fight has gone out of them you can talk to them, otherwise you can apply other techniques. (Interestingly, the resultant movement of the attacker is similar to that of the opening moves of Tekki Shodan / Nihanchi.)

{turn side on facing east} ...
{simultaneously do side kick and back fist southwards} ...
[{land into knife hand facing north} ...
^] {knife hand} ...
^ [{knife hand} ...
^ / {spear hand}

This combination reminds me of a famous story told about Itosu. Funakoshi describes it as follows in [MyWay]:

"Itosu was so well trained that his entire body seemed to be invulnerable. Once, as he was about to enter a restaurant in Naha's amusement center, a sturdy young man attacked him from the rear, aiming a hearty blow at his side. But the latter, without even turning, hardened the muscle of his stomach so that the blow glanced off [and grabbed] the right wrist of his assailant. Still without turning his head, he calmly dragged the man inside the restaurant. There, he ordered the frightened waitresses to bring food and wine. Still holding the man's wrist with his right hand, he took a sip of the wine from the cup that he held in his left hand, and then pulled his assailant around in front of him and for the first time had a look at him. After a moment, he smiled and said, "I don't know what your grudge against me could be, but let's have a drink together!" The young man's astonishment at this behavior can easily be imagined."

This time you are being attacked from behind. You take a big step back {side kick} and reach behind, grabbing your attacker {back fist southwards}. Using your Itosu-like power that you have developed during your karate training you haul your attacker in front of you (or equally drag yourself behind!) and soften them up with a few knife hands to the neck and body. You then firmly grab them (either their clothes or their neck) {spear hand} and ask them if they would like to join you for a drink.

I have shown a grab to the clothes in the picture. Firstly, a single hand grab to the neck is easy to escape from. More importantly, the intent is to subdue your attacker; to control them without them feeling their life is in danger so they decide not to fight any further. Whether this is a sensible strategy will depend on the situation. It is unlikely to be sensible if your attacker is drugged up. Either way, this move does bring up the topic of how to end a fight. If it can be ended without yourself or the attacker ending up in hospital, that is a bonus.

The common lesson of these two opening combinations is to manipulate a potentially bad situation to your advantage. Rather than turning to face your attacker, as they would expect, you attack to the side or behind to take your attacker by surprise and seize the initiative.

<270 E [{knife hand} ... >45 SE] {knife hand}

This combination is the same as the combination at the end of Heian Shodan. Having just shown us three straight on knife hands, it is telling us that taking up an angle to your attacker is actually preferable, for the reasons we discussed earlier. When this kata was the first kata in the series this would have been new advice.

There are three similar combinations on this section of the kata. To start with:

<90 S {large scooping motion with right arm into side block,
　　　left fist ends on hip}...
^ {front kick} ...
{reverse punch body}

The previous combination with the knife hands informed us that taking an angle to your attacker is desirable. This combination tells you one way of doing that. Your right arm goes under your attacker's guard and then grabs the outside of their right arm. You take a big step forward {front kick} and then attack from there {reverse punch body} (most likely changing the angle that you punch).

The movements in this first combination are very exaggerated. The combination is repeated again with slightly less exaggerated movements.

The set of combinations is completed by a reinforced side block.

The actual movements involved in executing this reinforced side block are actually the same as the previous two combinations, just much more minimalist. It is this quick, minimalist type movement you are aiming for. Not only is this set of combinations teaching you how to take an angle to your attacker, it is also telling you that to practice techniques you should start with exaggerated moves, and then refine them until they become fluid and optimal. This is also great advice for learning to ski!

<270 W {downward block} ...
>45 NW {upper block}

Initially this seems a rather dull end to the kata. But it encapsulates the katas two main themes. That is, if you are shorter than your attacker you can turn the situation to your advantage by angling your attack upwards under the jaw. It's turning an apparent disadvantage into an advantage using an angle.

This is an important consideration for a self-defence system. Height, weight and power all give a person advantage in a fight situation. Malicious attackers tend not to pick on people who are taller and bulkier than them, instead picking on people who are shorter and lighter. (As such, self-defence systems designed solely for big, strong people protecting themselves against smaller, weaker people are uncommon.) This combination is therefore an important lesson for self-defence.

As we know, Itosu put this kata first in the Pinan series and Funakoshi swapped it to the second kata because the other is easier to learn. Itosu must have also realised that Pinan Shodan (Heian Nidan) is harder than Pinan Nidan (Heian Shodan), so the question arises, why did he put the two katas in the order he did?

This kata is about principles and tactics that need to be considered before engaging in striking. You want to consider how to turn the fight situation to your advantage and position yourself for the best outcome. Hence the lessons of this kata need to be considered in a fight situation before you move on to enacting the striking lessons contained in Pinan Nidan (Heian Shodan). This is likely the reason Itosu put the harder kata first. He put the katas in "fight order" rather than difficulty order.

Note also that this kata contains a number of kicks, but in this bunkai they are demoted to "large step" or "important step". Many of the steps in the kata become small shuffles in a practical situation to adjust position relative to the attacker. The more important steps that are worth highlighting and worth separate discussion are represented by kicks.

Heian Sandan
Up and over

Karate is seen by many as primarily a punching and kicking art. But there is more to it than that, as I hope to show in this chapter. To help me with this I have enlisted some backup from Funakoshi's [Kyōhan] and Sensei Patrick McCarthy's [Bubishi].

= N ...
<90 W [{side block in back stance} ...
{move right foot beside of left foot,
       left arm downward block, right arm side block} ...
{left arm side block, right arm downward block}

In [Kyōhan], Funakoshi describes the double blocks as first defending against a simultaneous hand and leg attack from the attacker, immediately followed by another arm and leg attack from the attacker.

There are a number of problems with this "official" explanation. Firstly, that's some impressive skill from our attacker, especially as karate mostly assumes defence against an untrained attacker. Also, the kata appears to show two double blocks (four blocks in total) when our rules tell us there are no blocks in kata.

So, we need to work out what Funakoshi would have told us if he had trusted us with the secret knowledge.

We've just had a kata that has dealt with striking left, right and centre, and even up. There is little more the katas need to say about that. It's not a kicking move, so what other aspect of fighting could it relate to?

Luckily browsing through the Bubishi [Bubishi] gives as a clue. Here we find this image:

"Four horses on the loose" vs "Tiger pulling down a bear" from bottom of page 273 of [Bubishi]

And in [Kyōhan] we have these images:

"Kata-Sha-Rin" from [Kyōhan]

"Gyaku-Zuchi" from [Kyōhan]

In fact, Funakoshi has a whole section on Nage-Waza – throwing techniques. This combination represents grabbing an attacker's leg and up-ending them. This is a general principle and can be used in a number of different positions. As such it doesn't represent a single technique, but a principle.

In this particular scenario, the attacker is rotated in the direction shown in the kata because it moves the attacker's hand that is free to punch away from you.

So hopefully you're comfortable saying this combination can represent a throw. We've previously had an entire kata on pre-engagement considerations and an entire kata on striking. Is Heian Sandan an entire kata on throwing? Let's find out.

The first move in the northerly direction is simply:

    <90 N [{reinforced side block}

This can be used when the attacker is standing close, perhaps in a provocative, intimidating manner. You place your left leg behind their right leg and push them over. A simple but effective move.

The second move in the northerly direction is part of a sequence:

> ^ / {spear hand}
> {bring left foot to right foot while rotating body anti-clockwise,
> back of right hand on right hip, left hand under right armpit} ...
> {continue rotating anti-clockwise into horse stance
> with left arm hammer strike} ...
> {bring right leg forwards into forward stance and punch body}

This combination clearly shows a body rotation. Many karateka take such a rotation as an indication that the moves might represent a throw. If the combination represents a throw, then the spear hand is unlikely to be a strike. It could be a grab, or it could represent threading the arm between the attacker's left arm and body. The horizontal hammer fist continues the rotating motion and could be holding some part of the attacker.

The combination has all the characteristics of the Judo throw "O-goshi". This is one of the first throws taught to Judo students. Funakoshi shows a similar throw in [Kyōhan] called "Tani-Otoshi".

"Tani-Otoshi" from [Kyōhan]

What hasn't been explained is why the right hand is placed on the right hip in the second step and why the left hand is under the elbow in the spear hand.

For this we need to remember the earlier Advance rule 7, "Touching your own body in kata indicates that you are touching part of your opponent". The right hand on the hip is because in the throw the right hand goes around the attacker's back and is placed on their hip. The left hand under the right elbow on the spear hand is because in the throw the left hand grabs the attacker's right elbow. (The left hand is under the right armpit during the rotation when the right hand is on the hip because the attacker is effectively under your right arm during the throw.)

You may have noticed that the last step and punch in this sequence isn't actually part of the throw {bring right leg forwards into forward stance and punch body}. A counter to the throw is for the person being thrown to slide over the thrower's hip and land in front. To recover from this, the thrower moves their right leg from behind the person being thrown to in front and pushes them over (application photo not shown).

There are two techniques demonstrated on this leg. The moves for the first one are:

{start facing south with a ready stance feet position and fists on hips} ...
{raise the right leg} ...
{step forwards and pivot into a horse stance} ...
{the right arm swings out with the elbow slightly bent and fist to head height}

The technique is repeated three times on alternating sides.

Once again, looking at the Bubishi [Bubishi] gives us a clue:

"Going to fight with one knife" vs "Fighting alone at the gate of an official residence" from bottom page 283 from [Bubishi]

You grab the attacker's left wrist with your left hand. With your right leg step up and around to behind the attacker's left leg, then with your right arm, push them backwards over your leg.

The Bubishi shows the technique with your arm going over the attacker's arm to the neck, however it works equally well with your arm going under the attacker's arm to the chest and is a better fit if you are shorter than your attacker.

The second technique in this section is as follows:

{from horse stance with both fists on hips with elbows outwards} ...
{move both elbows to point backwards,
 with left hand closed and right hand open} ...
{slowly circle the right hand forwards and to the right, ending as if to
 show a "stop" sign to someone to your right} ...
{step forward with the left leg into forward stance facing south and
 punch body with the left arm}

This time we can look at Funakoshi's [Kyōhan] for guidance:

"Byo-bu Daoshi" from [Kyōhan] flipped horizontally

You grab the attacker's left wrist with your right hand {slowly circle the right hand forwards...}. This requires no power which is why the kata has this as a slow movement. You position your left leg behind the attacker and push them over {step forward with the left leg...}. Funakoshi calls this "Byo-bu Daoshi", but it is also very similar to Judo's beginner O-Soto-Gari throw.

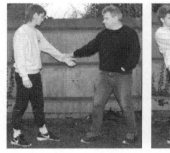

The last combination of the kata carries on from the punch of the previous combination:

{bring right foot to left foot, then to the right to shoulder width apart} ...
{twist the right foot anti-clockwise then move the left foot so that it ends up on the opposite side of the right foot, having turned the body 180° left} ...
{as the body turns, bring the left fist to left hip and right fist over left shoulder}

This is similar to the O-goshi hip throw except that the right hand goes to the attacker's left shoulder and the attacker is dropped over your right leg. This is the Judo throw, Tai-otoshi.

That completes Heian Sandan. I hope you are agreed that it can be seen as a kata all about throws and body drops intended to put your opponent on the ground.

Heian Yondan
On your feet!!!

Heian Yondan is a popular kata for bunkai enthusiasts to interpret. I suppose that is because it is the first kata of the series that isn't "obviously" punching and kicking.

So far we have seen that the kata series involves a kata on pre-fight considerations, a kata on punching, and a kata for throws and body drops. These echo the characteristic "lifecycle" of a fight (although you would hope that a fight would be resolved in your favour before all stage of the lifecycle have completed).

What would be the next phase in the fight lifecycle? One might think it is ground work. But is it? This is not an area typically associated with karate. To prove or disprove this hypothesis let's assume it is ground work until demonstrated otherwise.

The kata begins by raising the arms to the left in a back stance and then lowering the arms. The kata then involves raising the arms in a similar fashion on the right. It's this latter raising the arms on the right where this interpretation begins because the arm raise on the left only expresses part of the story.

Changing the viewing angle (looking west from the east), the part of the kata we want is this:

> {back stance towards the right, left hand open in front of the forehead, right hand open to the right of the head} ...
> {step forwards with left leg with arms in X block, right arm on top} ...
> {step forwards with reinforced side block}

To start testing the hypothesis that this is a ground technique, let's start face down on the floor – the most basic ground position.

The open left hand is moved above the head and the right arm and leg are moved to the right {...left hand open in front of the forehead...}. We push down with both hands and bring up our left leg {X block in forward stance}. We keep pushing on the ground and bring up our other (right leg) {reinforced side block} and move into a standing position. (If you are right-handed, with your right arm stronger than your left, you will likely find the mirror image of this sequence easier and more natural to perform, as hinted by the opening two moves of the kata that we skipped. That is, arms and left leg go to left side, then, while pushing up, bring up right leg, followed by bringing up left leg.)

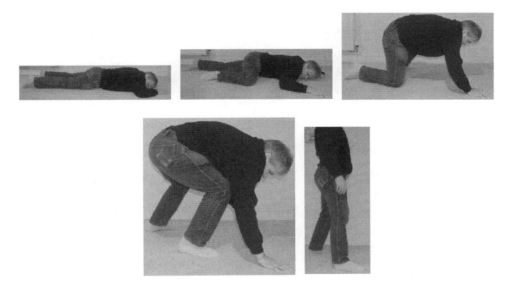

Thus the instruction of this combination would initially appear to be "if you end up on the ground, get up". This is good advice as you have much greater mobility and enhanced ability to escape if you are on your feet.

Let's look at the next combination:

> {bring the left foot to the side of the right foot, both fists on right hip} ...
> {simultaneously do left side kick and back fist to left} ...
> {land on left foot in forward stance with elbow strike}

How can we make this a ground scenario?

If we are on the ground, we may not be able to get up straight away. For example, if our attacker is near and about to jump on us. In that case, as the attacker comes round to attack, roll on to your side (hence the off-line kick) and do a kick to the groin or knee. Hopefully the attacker will lean forwards due to the kick, in which case grab their head with your arm and drag them to the ground.

That's two out of two ground techniques so far, but it could be coincidence. We need to continue.

Following the elbow strike of the previous combinations, we have the following:

{right hand open to forehead, left hand open out to left at hip height} ...
{without changing foot position, pivot hips 90° into forward stance with
    left leg forward, now with
    left hand open on forehead, and
    right open at head height with palm open and facing up} ...
{right leg does front kick but afterwards remains in chamber position as you
    bring right fist down, then towards you, then up, then forwards
    in a circular motion with left fist being 180° out of phase,
    ending with right hand back fist and left fist on hip,
    left leg directly behind right leg}

We haven't disproved that this kata is about ground techniques so far, so let's continue with that. The combinations in a kata ideally progress from presenting the best scenario and then cover increasingly bad situations. If this applies here, we need a situation with us on the ground in a worse situation than with the attacker standing over us.

One such situation is if both you and the attacker are laying side-by-side on the ground. In such a case we could strike the attacker laying next to us in the belly or groin {left hand open out to left at hip height} to encourage them to roll away from us. We then roll to our left so we are on our side {pivot hips 90° into forward stance}, our left hand is next to our head {left hand open on forehead} and our right hand is reaching over the attacker {right open at head height with palm open} to grab the attacker's right arm. The kata does a kick next, so we throw our leg over the attacker, so our legs are straddling them {right leg does front kick but afterwards remains in chamber position}. Finally, we pull against the attacker to raise ourselves into a standing position, bringing our left leg behind the attacker's back, to execute an arm lock {bring right fist … in a circular motion}.

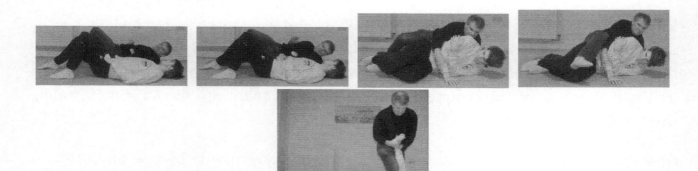

Despite this being a relatively long sequence, it does appear to correlate well with a ground technique, but there are still two more combinations remaining.

For the next combination:

    {turn 225° left into left leg back stance} …

    {hands raised up into an X block in front of the chest} …

    {rotate both fists and move fists to sides so backs of hands face you} …

    {kick with right leg into right leg forward stance} …

    {right fist punch body, left fist to hip} …

    {left fist punch body, right fist to hip}

Before we were on our back with the attacker to our side. To satisfy the kata progression we would anticipate finding ourselves in a worse predicament. For example, we are on our back as before but this time the attacker is sitting on top of us trying to strangle us.

We thread our hands between the attacker's arm {hands raised up into an X block} and grip his arms over the top {rotate both fists and move fists to sides}. We try to push the attacker to our right side (our 45° angle in the kata). To help with this we throw our right leg out to the right {kick with right leg}. The attacker will resist our attempt to push them off and so will push to our left. We take advantage of this by quickly pushing the attacker left by pushing with our right arm and pulling with our left {right fist punch body, left fist to hip}. We roll over and push with our left arm to raise ourselves into a standing position {left fist punch body, right fist to hip}.

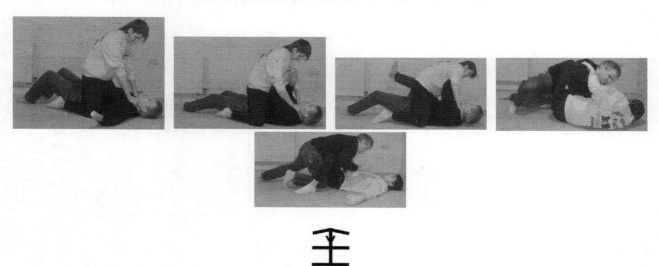

It would be a shame for this kata to have so much that works for ground techniques but fails on the final combination. But it still might. The final combination is:

S [{left reinforced side block} ...
^] {right reinforced side block} ...
^ [{left reinforced side block} ...
\ {right leg drops outwards so we end in forward stance,
    both fists raised in front of us at head height, backs of hands facing us} ...
{right leg raised up as if to front kick, fists on hips} ...
N [{twist around into left knife hand} ...
^] {step forward into right knife hand}

We've been on our back with the attacker on top of us. What could be worse than that? Has the kata run out of scenarios?

One option is the attacker is on top of us, but this time we are face down. How might this work?

We push up our right side using our reinforced left arm to try to push our attacker off {left reinforced side block}. This probably won't work and our attacker will resist it. So we quickly drop our right side down and push up on our left {right reinforced side block}. This may shake our attacker off, but if it doesn't we keep repeating the principle {left reinforced side block}. This is a standard rocking table escape technique. When we feel the attacker sliding off, we push up with both hands out front {both fists raised in front of us at head height} and bring our right leg forwards to stand up on {right leg raised up as if to front kick}. Once standing we rotate towards our attacker {twist around} and if they are still clinging on, shake them off {knife hand}.

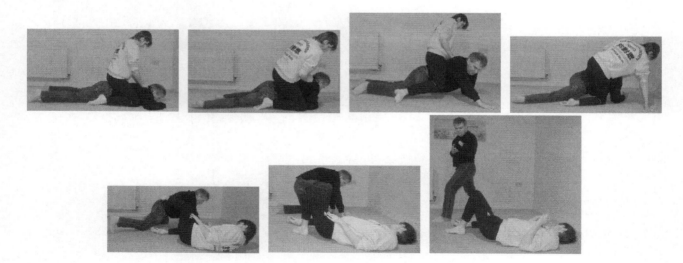

That appears to be a kata with five combinations that can be interpreted as ground fighting techniques, with each combination illustrating a scenario more undesirable than the previous. The kata itself fits into a sequence of katas that follow the lifecycle of a fight. Interestingly, the Korean Palgue kata series I originally studied, whose creators studied under Funakoshi, also has a similar ground fighting techniques kata (Palgue Yuk Jang), suggesting that ground techniques weren't alien to the karateka of that era. So, despite karate not usually being associated with ground techniques, it's finally reasonable to accept that this is in fact a kata about ground techniques!

Even more, it's reasonable to start entertaining the idea that the whole kata series is a coherent syllabus with each kata detailing techniques for different phases of the fight lifecycle.

Heian Godan
What's left?

We have one more kata, but we have covered most aspects of the fight lifecycle. What more is there to cover?

One thing we haven't fully covered is how to end a fight. Recall that in Heian Nidan, rather than knocking his attacker out, Itosu was able to end a confrontation by restraining him. Thus it suggests that knocking out the attacker might not be the only way to end a fight. What other options might there be?

{from ready position (yoi)}
{left foot steps out to side block in back stance} ...
{right arm punches to left} ...
{right foot brought up to left foot, right fist to right hip,
    left fist angled in front}

When an attacker grabs us, we grab their right elbow with our left hand {left foot steps out to side block in back stance}. We grab their right wrist with our right hand {right arm punches to left}. We position ourselves behind their elbow {right foot brought up to left foot} and push their elbow forwards into an arm lock {right fist to right hip, left fist angled in front}.

This is a basic restraining move that I'm told is often taught to police officers. Whether it is wise to opt for such a restraint to end a fight depends on the situation and is a topic left for someone else's book.

The combination following consists solely of a reinforced side block:

This may look a simple and inconsequential move but in this context it represents the first move you will find on a traditional jujitsu syllabus. When you are grabbed by an attacker you reach over to the non-thumb side of their hand with your fingers on their palm and then rotate their arm over into a lock.

The next two combinations are quite long and a situation when the attacker doesn't play fair.

] {reinforced side block} (photo not shown) ...
^ \ {fists down in X block} ...
\ {retract then raise hands in X block, hands open, back-to-back} ...
\ {twist hands!} ...
\ {both fists to right hip} ...
\ {slowly extend out left arm} ...
^ / {step forward with punch body} ...
{fold arms, raise up right leg, rotate 270° left to land in horse stance,
    body faces east, head south} ...
{fold arms, left under right, then right fist to hip,
    left open hand slowly extended to north} ...
{crescent kick with right leg to open left hand}

In this scenario the attacker brings a stick to a fist fight. Or in the Okinawan karate case, a Bo (AKA Bo-staff) to a fist fight.

As this sequence is long, I will interleave the bunkai pictures with the explanation.

Wanting to strike us with the bo, the attacker raises the staff such that the bottom end does an upward striking motion. This is blocked with the downward X block {fists down in X block}. The attacker then rotates the bo to strike downwards. The bo is blocked and grabbed {raise hands in X block, hands open, back-to-back} {twist hands!}. The bo is pulled by both hands to the right hip {both fists to right hip}. The left hand is extended along the bo towards the attacker {slowly extend out left arm} (This is a slow move in the kata as it requires no force).

The next steps attempt to twist the bo out of the attacker's hands. Step forwards and twist the bo anti-clockwise in the horizontal plane {step forward with punch body}. With great force, push the right end of the bo upwards and rotate your body anti-clockwise, pulling the bo out of the attacker's hands {rotate 270° left}.

Pull the bo round the body {left open hand slowly extended to north}. Place the right foot on the bo and push it to the ground, out of reach of the attacker {crescent kick with right leg}.

The kata move after the crescent kick is an elbow strike.

However, looking at it from this angle is not helpful as all the detail is on the far side. Therefore, the following pictures show the kata from the opposite angle to the previous set of pictures (from west looking east rather than east looking west. Looking at the pictures, north is to the left).

{elbow strike in horse stance} ...
>90 N {reinforced side block with left foot crossed directly behind right foot} ...
<90 W {step left foot south slightly, raise reinforced side block into the air} ...
<180 E {jump 180° left, landing with left foot crossed directly behind right,
knees bent, hands in downward X block, right fist over left} ...
>90 S {turn to right with reinforced side block}

This time a bo or shorter stick is being pointed directly at us. Once again, as there are a number of pictures for this bunkai, I'll interleave the description and the pictures.

We grab the bo with our right hand and then grab the bo with the left hand from underneath, a forearms length nearer the attacker {elbow strike in horse stance}.

We once again attempt to twist the bo out of the attacker's hands, this time by raising up the right hand to put the bo in a vertical position and pushing towards the attacker {reinforced side block with left foot crossed directly behind right foot}. With both hands we push up and pull away from the attacker {step left foot south slightly, raise reinforced side block into the air}. With great force we yank the bo out of the attacker's hands, rotating our body so that it is between the bo and the attacker {jump 180° left}. (The intention is not to actually jump as in the kata. The attacker restraining the bo prevents us from leaving the ground. However, we have to use such force that if the attacker wasn't restraining us, we would end up jumping into the air.) We finish by moving the bo away from the attacker so they can't re-grab it {turn to right with reinforced side block}.

For the next combination (Photos taken looking from the east to the west, north is to the right):

\ {Step forwards into left forward stance,
 right hand open strikes to groin height,
 left hand closed over right shoulder} ...
{right hand pulled back behind the head,
 left hand downward block over left knee} ...
{left foot pulled back to right foot,

This combination is for when a weapon such as a bo or naginata is held in a pre-attack position. The attacker holds the bo with their right hand by their right hip and their left hand in front of them. To disarm the attacker, your left hand is placed near the top of the bo and then you step forwards with your left leg and grab the bo low down with your right hand. You twist the bo 180° to partially break the attacker's grip and then pull the bo backwards to break the grip completely.

For the final combination:

{Both feet are together pointing the your left so you are side-on to the enemy,
   left arm is raised and covering your forehead,
      right arm is in an L shape with hand open in front of you} ...
{Step forward with right leg into a forward stance,
   right hand (closed) over left shoulder,
      left hand (open) to groin area} ...
{Left hand is closed and pulls back over left shoulder,
   right hand does downward block}

Here the attacker is holding a bo or spear above their shoulder. Similar to the earlier technique, the bo is grabbed and you use your left hand to push the bo down and to the opposite side of the attacker, partially breaking their grip. The bo is then twisted back 180° to fully break the grip.

That completes the bunkai for the Heian Godan. A kata that continues the theme of having a kata per fighting situation. In this case the theme is about locks and dealing with weapons. It shows how traditional karate includes aspects today considered to be partitioned off into jujitsu and kobudo.

Some have speculated that Heian Godan was developed by someone other than Itosu because it is stylistically different. We can see here that the reason it may be stylistically different is because it describes techniques for a very different situation.

Conclusion

Congratulations, you have now looked at the applications of all the katas in the Heian series.

Most of the techniques presented are simple and unlikely to be considered "Best of Class" by truly advanced martial artists. The syllabus doesn't have many advanced techniques such as arm locks and close quarter grappling. Some readers might even be disappointed by the simplicity of the techniques presented here. But personally I think this is a strength. A simple technique well applied in a moment of crisis by someone who might not have trained for as long as they would have liked is better than a complicated technique applied badly.

The separate katas for each combat scenario means you can more easily select a suitable combination to execute depending on the combat situation. For example, you can think, "I'm now in a close quarter standing situation so something from Heian Sandan is likely what I need." This is an easier process than if techniques from all scenarios were jumbled across all of the katas.

So I hope that you will agree with me that the Heian series is an excellent beginners' self-defence syllabus and shouldn't be looked at simply as a form of kids' aerobics [NotKids].

Ultimately there is no way of knowing how close the syllabus presented in this book matches the applications intended by Itosu and the other kata authors. I hope they are close. All the pieces fit together so well that it's hard to believe it is a coincidence. Like when doing a Sudoku puzzle, if the numbers work for the horizontal, vertical and block then you can feel confident that you have a good answer without someone having to tell you you are right.

If they are close to the original intent, or the original authors intended something similar but different, I think we should have great admiration for the genius of those authors. The nature of a kata, such as the kata embusen and the limitations on the number of steps in each direction, imposes considerable constraints on what can be conveyed, and yet the authors have been able to describe a comprehensive fighting system containing not only striking techniques but throws and even ground techniques.

The katas also work wonderfully as tools for practicing the basics of karate with their migration from using simple stances and techniques to more advanced ones, and, as we know, they are a fantastic resource for improving physical fitness, conditioning and flexibility.

By now I feel I should have convinced you of one of two things. Either these katas form a comprehensive fight syllabus, or that you can associate any application you like to a kata if you have enough will! I hope it is the former.

Before I leave you I just want to re-emphasise that this is just "an" interpretation of the katas. Obviously I'm inclined to think it is a good one. But it's important to keep looking at the katas to see what they can teach us. At their most abstract the katas can be looked at as a series of knots in hankies to act as reminders for what an instructor can teach their students. We must be ever mindful of the risk of a good bunkai interpretation becoming the "one true bunkai" with the result that it limits what we can learn from a kata. If a bunkai for a set of kata moves works for you, and the kata helps you remember and practice those moves, then it is a good bunkai, even if that application never occurred to the creators of the kata.

I hope you have enjoyed this journey into a deep description of the Heian series of katas.

If you enjoyed this book, please leave a review on Amazon and help spread the knowledge to other karateka. Many thanks.

References

[5Rings] Musashi, Miyamoto (translated by Thomas Cleary), *The Book of Five Rings*, Shabhala Publications, Inc, ISBN 978-1-59030-248-4, 1993

[Abernethy] https://iainabernethy.co.uk/content/different-terms-used-bunkai

[ArtWar] Sun Tzu, *The Art of War,* Pax Librorum Publishing House, ISBN 978-0-9811626-1-4, 2009

[Bubishi] Patrick McCarthy, *Bubishi – The Classic Manual of Combat,* Tuttle Publishing, ISBN 978-4-8053-1384-8, 2016.

[Bunkai] https://en.wikipedia.org/wiki/Bunkai

[Enkamp] https://www.youtube.com/watch?v=q9kS4nOXPCI

[Funakoshi] https://en.wikipedia.org/wiki/Gichin_Funakoshi

[Itosu] https://en.wikipedia.org/wiki/Ank%C5%8D_Itosu

[Jutsu] Iain Abernethy. *Bunkai-Jutsu: The Practical Application of Karate Kata*. Kindle Edition, ISBN 978-0953893218.

[Kyōhan] Funakoshi, Gichin (translated by Harumi Suzuki-Johnston). *Karate Dō Kyōhan: Master Text for the Way of the Empty-Hand*. San Diego, CA: Neptune Publications, 2012.

[MyWay] Funakoshi, Gichin. *Karate-do: My Way Of Life*

[NotKids]   https://www.youtube.com/watch?v=DS5nSNwQ5Os

[Palgue]   Pete Cordell, *Palgue Bunkai*, https://www.amazon.co.uk/dp/B08FP25J84/

[Pinan]   https://en.wikipedia.org/wiki/Pinan

[Rules]   https://en.wikipedia.org/wiki/Kaisai_no_genri

[Strike]   Iain Abernethy, https://iainabernethy.co.uk/article/no-first-attack-karate

[Twenty]   Funakoshi, Gichin, and Genwa Nakasone. *The Twenty Guiding Principles of Karate: The Spiritual Legacy of the Master*. Kodansha USA, 2012.